Originally published as *Wow! Onder de aardkorst. Reis naar de kern van onze planeet*
in Belgium and the Netherlands by Clavis Uitgeverij, 2019
English translation from the Dutch by Clavis Publishing Inc., New York

Visit us on the Web at www.clavis-publishing.com.

Wow! Underneath the Earth's Crust. Trip to the Core of Our Planet written and illustrated by Mack van Gageldonk

ISBN 978-1-60537-805-3

This book was printed in August 2022 at Nikara, M. R. Štefánika 858/25, 963 01 Krupina, Slovakia.

First Edition
10 9 8 7 6 5 4 3 2 1

Clavis Publishing supports the First Amendment and celebrates the right to read.

Previous page: Tham Lot cave, Thailand

Trip to the Core of Our Planet

UNDERNEATH THE EARTH'S CRUST

Mack

Clavis

NEW YORK

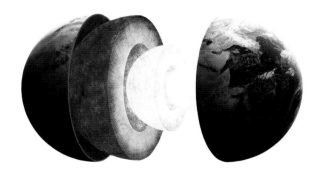

The Inside of Our Planet

From space, the earth looks like a beautiful ball of white clouds, blue oceans, and earth–toned bodies of land. But on the inside, the earth looks very different. Imagine digging a hole all the way to the center of the earth! It would be over 3,728 miles deep!

If you traveled to the center of the earth, you'd encounter peculiar animals, caves, gemstones, fossils, thermal springs, and boiling rock. No one has ever done it! And that's what makes it so exciting! Will you come on this incredible journey?

As Hot As the Sun

Although the ground beneath your feet is strong enough to hold people, towns, cities, states, and even entire countries—it's smaller than you might realize. Indeed, **you're walking on a very thin layer.**

We call this thin layer the earth's crust. If you compare it to an apple, the earth's crust is even thinner than the apple's skin. Just beneath the earth's crust is the mantle which is made of a hot, thick, liquid rock called magma. The earth's crust floats on the magma. In the very center of the earth is the core, which is even hotter than the magma at nearly 10,832 degrees Fahrenheit. That's as hot as the sun! The outer core is comprised of liquid, and the middle is solid.

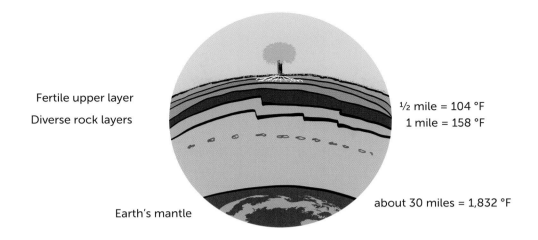

Fertile upper layer

Diverse rock layers

Earth's mantle

½ mile = 104 °F

1 mile = 158 °F

about 30 miles = 1,832 °F

Life in the Earth's Crust

The earth's outer crust has a thickness of 19 to 44 miles. Life can exist in the earth's crust, but not beneath it. Beneath the earth's crust is 1,832 degrees Fahrenheit, which prevents any possibility of life.

Inside the earth's crust, the soil is also very hot. Within a ½ mile, the temperature rises to 104 degrees Fahrenheit—as hot as the tropical sun! At the 1-mile mark, it's 158 degrees Fahrenheit! That's why plants and animals can't survive beneath the earth's crust.

The top of the earth's crust contains fertile soil such as sand and clay. These soils are friendly and welcoming to plant life. Beneath the soil, you'll find rock layers formed by volcanic eruptions. In the course of millions of years, one layer grows on top of another, which leads to various layers of stone in the earth's crust.

Me, too!

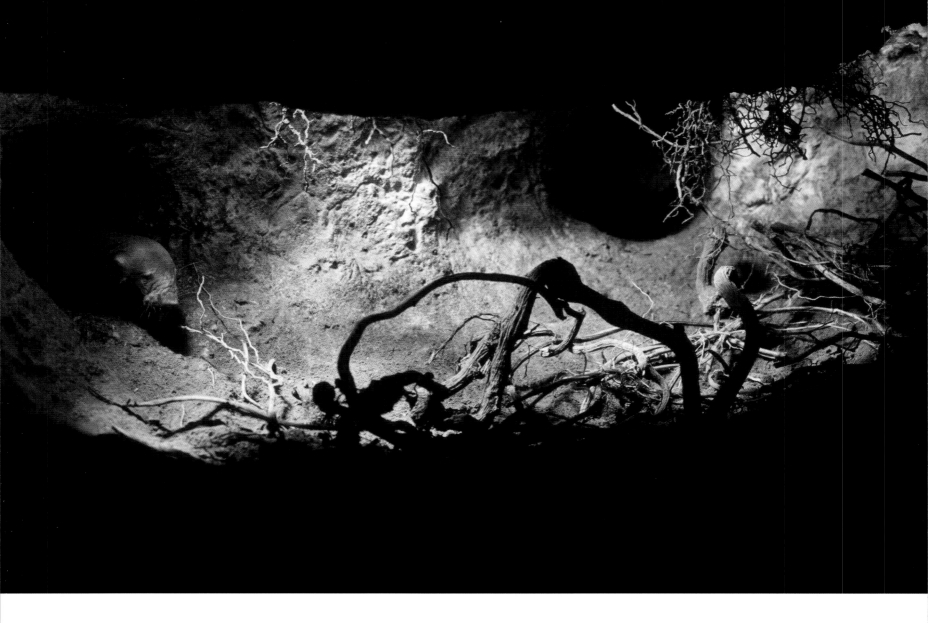

The Ground is Full of Life

Just below the earth's surface—where it's pitch-dark—burrow animals such as **mice, marmots, and rabbits** live. Their underground houses often have several rooms—even a room for their babies! This way, predators are kept at a distance.

Molehills

Moles live primarily underground. **Moles** are always searching for juicy worms—their favorite!

Good Diggers

Many worms, like their enemy the mole, live underground. And like moles, **worms** are excellent diggers. They can expand and contract all the pieces of their bodies separately. This way, they can dig small tunnels through which water can pass and plants can grow.

Trees, mushrooms, and plants grow in the top layer of the earth's crust. Sometimes their roots stick deep into the ground and take food and water from the soil. Scientists have discovered that trees can even "talk" to each other with their roots! If one tree is ill, the other trees share of their own strength and health—like medicine.

It's dark here.

Here, too!

Here, too!

The Wonderful World of Caves

Have you ever wanted to walk underground? You can—in caves! In **a stalactite or a stalagmite cave,** you'll find the most beautiful underground corridors and rooms, created by rainwater. Rainwater falls on the earth and sinks into the ground. Each drop absorbs a grain of stone, and then the grain sticks together like clay. Sometimes entire columns are created like this!

Stalactite and stalagmite caves develop very slowly, so you must be really patient. Sometimes you have to wait millions of years!

Tham Lot cave, Thailand

Shining in Caves

Animals like to hide in caves. **Bats,** for example, prefer sleeping in caves. They hang from the ceiling with their eyes closed. In the cave of Waitomo in New Zealand, you'll find **glowworms,** or larvae of beetles. They make a nest of threads, just like silkworms do, and then they radiate blue light from the underside of their bodies. Flies are attracted to the blue light and stick to the glowworm's slimy threads. The glowworms enjoy eating the flies.

Stalactite

Dripstones can take on many forms. One of the most famous forms is the stalactite. A stalactite is **an icicle** that **hangs** from the ceiling of the stalactite cave. Water droplets join with pieces of dissolved gravel from the ceiling. They grow very slowly—sometimes only 39 inches every thousand years!

Stalagmite

Dripstones not only hang from the ceiling, but they also grow from the ground. A **dripstone pillar** is called a stalagmite. Like a stalactite, a stalagmite is formed by falling water. When a drop of water falls on something hard, it bursts, leaving gravel behind.

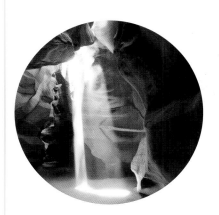

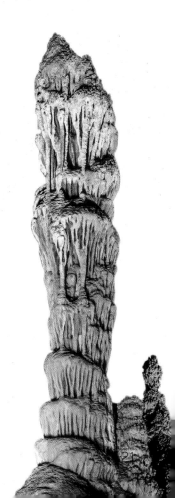

In the United States, you can visit the **Antelope Canyon,** which used to be desert land. After thousands of years, the wind smoothed and compressed the sand, resulting in the formation of a gorge. The Antelope Canyon is 1,312 feet long and 131 feet deep.

Here you can find treasures in the earth.

Here, too!

Treasures Deep in the Earth

Treasures like rocks and minerals lie deep within the earth. Through them, houses are fueled and ships and planes are built. Some minerals are easily accessed, but not all. Iron is especially difficult to extract.

Minerals are excavated through deep tunnels or **mines.** Most mines are up to several hundred yards deep. The deepest mines reach up to 2 miles! Because the working conditions are extreme, mines are often cooled down with ice and fans.

A Life under the Ground

In the past, miners used pickaxes and transported minerals in baskets or trolleys. Some mining corridors were many miles long. Miners spent much of their lives underground. In recent days, caves are mined by machines.

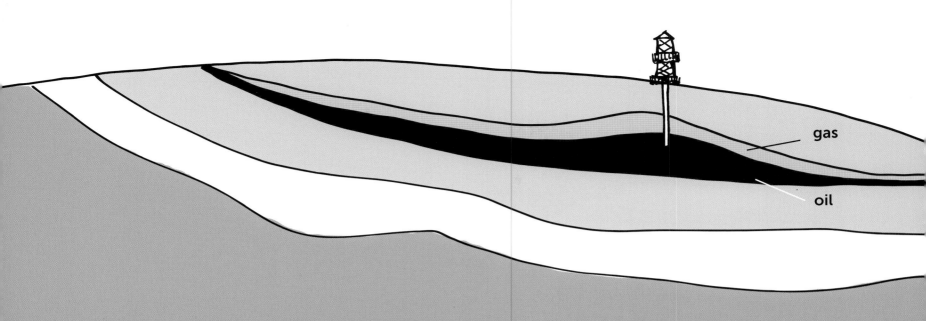

gas

oil

Digging for Petroleum and Natural Gas

Millions of years ago, most of the earth was covered in water. Small animals like plankton died and rested on the ocean floor. In time, layers formed and turned into a tar-like substance. The warmth of the earth melted the substance into an oil, which eventually evaporated. The end result was natural gas. Plastic, petrol, and heating gas are made from crude oil and natural gas.

Sometimes mining entails extracting substances from large chunks of stone. This is true with **iron** and **steel.** Thousands of years ago, people melted iron from stone to make arrowheads. Now this is done in factories, and the iron is used to make strong steel. Steel is very useful in the construction of ships.

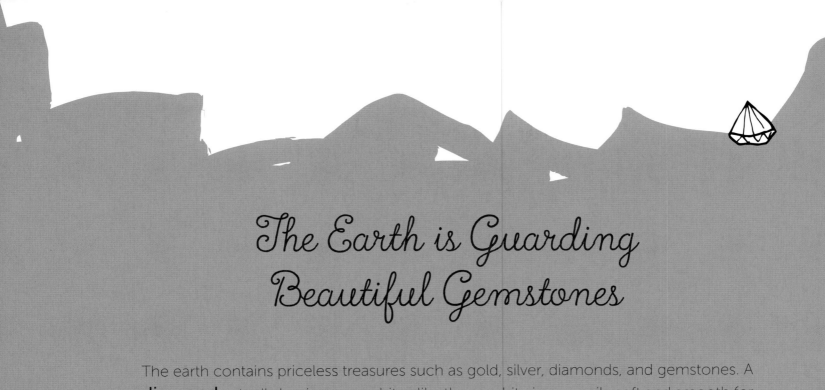

The Earth is Guarding Beautiful Gemstones

The earth contains priceless treasures such as gold, silver, diamonds, and gemstones. A **diamond** actually begins as graphite—like the graphite in a pencil—soft and smooth for writing. Deep in the earth, heavy earth layers press on pieces of graphite. When completely compressed in heat, the graphite transforms into a diamond.

But how does a diamond get to the surface of the earth? This happens through volcanic eruption. Boiling hot lava erupts from the center of the earth, leaving treasures (diamonds!) all over the ground. Did you know that diamonds are the hardest stones on earth? They're extremely rare and expensive. They're often made into jewelry and even into drills at the dentist!

Dinosaur Remains

In addition to finding beautiful stones and useful minerals in the earth's crust, you can also find dinosaurs! Not the living kind, of course, but **fossils.** Fossils are the **remains,** or **prints,** of animals that died a long time ago. Sometimes the animals are compressed within layers of the earth, and a stone imprint remains. Fossils help us to consider what dinosaurs looked like millions of years ago.

Searching for Gold

Gold is extremely expensive. This is because it's often hidden underground. But sometimes gold can be found on the earth's surface—often in clear, calm rivers, where water has washed it clean of dirt. Gold miners from all over the world walk through rivers with sieves, in hopes of getting rich. With a bit of luck, they'll find tiny pieces of gold, and if they're really lucky, a nugget!

One Stone is Harder Than the Other

Gemstones are not only beautiful, but also very hard. With a knife, you can make a scratch on glass, but not on a **gemstone.** This is how you can distinguish imposter diamonds and quartz from the real thing.

Stones in All Colors

Stones can be found in all kinds of colors, and some stones can even be multi–colored. This happens when another metal joins with a stone. For example, iron can make the crystals in an amethyst turn purple, and copper can make azurite turn blue.

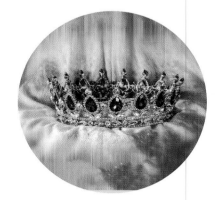

Have you ever noticed the crowns of princesses, kings, and queens? Their crowns are often made of gold and stones. And those **crown jewels** come out of the ground! From scarlet rubies to sparkling diamonds . . . almost all of them have grown out of a tiny fragment inside of the earth.

I dive
into the deep.

A Dive in the Deep Sea

To descend very deep into the earth, you don't have to dig a hole! You can climb into a submarine! You can see large schools of fish in all the colors of the rainbow, and find mysterious caves. The deeper you dive, the darker and more exciting it becomes . . .

At a depth of a few hundred yards, everything turns pitch-black. It's hard to tell if plants are growing or if fish are swimming. But every now and then, you'll see moving lights. These are luminous fish! They have blinking lights to attract mates and fend off enemies.

Mountains Continue underneath Sea Level

The deepest place on earth is the **Mariana Trench**. It's a gap between Japan and Indonesia that's more than 6 miles deep. That's deeper than the height of Mount Everest, the tallest mountain on earth! It's impossible to survive at such depths due to extreme water pressure.

Luminous Ballet Dancers

Have you ever seen a jellyfish? They're very beautiful, and also very dangerous. A **jellyfish** can cause great injury with their tentacles. Like the other light-up fish, jellyfish can also light up—but in fluorescent colors! As they slowly dance through the sea, they look like luminous ballet dancers.

Deep Divers

Did you know that sperm whales have a useful diving trick? In their large head is a fat hump, and when blood travels to that hump, they grow heavier. This helps them dive deeper as they search for their favorite food: colossal squid. They swim at a depth of 2 miles. Colossal squid can measure more than 33 feet in length and weigh more than 220 pounds! **Sperm whales** love to feast on them.

The deeper you dive, the stranger the animals appear. There are fish so thin, they almost fall apart! There are spiders that can grow up to 2 feet long! And in thick layers of mud, you can even find fish with legs! There are also fish with eyes on the tops of their heads. The lantern fish has a light on top of its head for luring and catching smaller fish.

I blow steam
from the earth.

I squirt!

I bubble!

Hverir, Iceland

Bubbling and Squirting above a Thin Earth's Crust

In a few places on earth, you can see a special phenomenon: geysers. **Geysers** are natural fountains that can squirt water to high heights. You can find them at Yellowstone National Park in the United States. Because of the earth's thin surface and the hot magma beneath it, collected rain water bubbles to a boil. As the pressure increases, the water expands and erupts. The most famous geyser is **Old Faithful.** Several times each day, it sprays water up to 184 feet high.

Having a Nice Bath in a Thermal Spring

Near the Japanese city of **Nagano,** you can find hot thermal springs. In the winter, when it's freezing and snowing outside, the water basin continues to steam and never freezes.

The water's heat source is deep in the earth. Boiling magma heats the entire pool. Many people love to bathe in hot springs. In Nagano, the bath is also popular with a **group of macaques.** Rain or sun, the monkeys know exactly where they can find a lovely, hot bath.

A Painting of Hot Water

Yellowstone National Park has volcanic activity below its surface. The **bright colors** of its hot springs are the result of **bacteria**-killing water in the center of the lake. This gives the water its beautiful blue color. In the surrounding rings, the bacteria produce orange and yellow substances. The mixing with the blue creates the green color.

The Sea Squirts and Whistles

Not all fountains are geysers. In the sea, you can find another kind of **fountain.** When the seawater flows into the cavity of a cave, it can't travel far without an escape, such as a blowhole. When the flooded water forces itself through the hole, it erupts into the air as an impressive fountain.

Mud Bath

When mud is heated by the earth, a mud bath, or **mud volcano,** is created. In Azerbaijan, there are 350 mud volcanoes! The large bubbles burst into a simmering, gray soup–like substance.

Iceland is an island that grows about an inch each year. This is because one side of the country is slowly drifting away from the other. This means that a hole, or fracture, exists in the middle of the island. Magma flows from the depths of the earth and warms the landscape. Here you'll find many geysers, which are **bubbling, simmering, and spraying.**

Me, too!

Pingvellir, Iceland

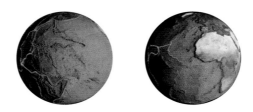

Earth Plates Rub Together

Did you know that the earth's crust isn't fixed to the earth? It's true! It actually moves! This is because the inner part of the earth, the magma, is liquid, and the earth's crust floats on top of it. Each part of the earth's crust floats in a different direction. Some tectonic plates float towards each other, while others float away from each other. Because the plates are heavy, they start to vibrate and tremble as they collide or rub against each other. This causes **earthquakes** and **volcanic eruptions.** The shocks cause cracks in the earth's layers, through which the hot magma is released. Many volcanoes can be found at the interfaces of the floating earth plates. The most notorious area where this happens runs from America to Asia and is also called **The Ring of Fire.**

Two tectonic plates drift apart.

Two tectonic plates move under each other.

The Richter Scale

The strength of an earthquake is indicated by a number between one and ten. These are numbers on the Richter scale. On this scale, the force is ten times stronger with each step. So, an earthquake with a force of five on the Richter scale is ten times stronger than a quake with a force of four, and a hundred times stronger than a quake with a force of three. At force five, the glasses in your cupboard start shaking, and at force six, your whole house is shaking. The strongest earthquake took place in Chile in 1960 with a force of 9.5 on the Richter scale.

The Earth's Crust Moves Apart

On top of the floating earth's crust, plates collide with each other, rub against each other, and drift away from each other. This most commonly occurs below sea level, but it can also occur on land. When the moving plates tear apart the earth, deep **gorges** remain.

The Earth Folds Double

As earth plates collide, **mountains** are formed. Did you know that mountains are actually ripples and folds in the earth's crust? They're created by two tectonic plates pushing against each other.

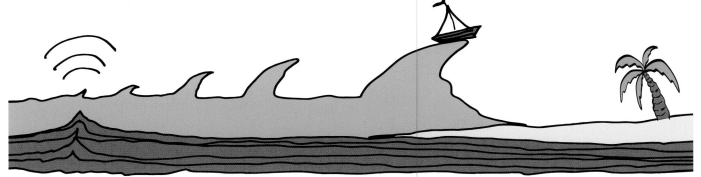

Earthquakes also occur at the bottom of the sea. When this happens, a **tsunami** is imminent. The vibrations in the earth's crust cause a ripple in the water, creating a huge wave. When the tsunami wave reaches the beach, it can be up to 33 feet and flood an entire city.

The hot magma flows out here.

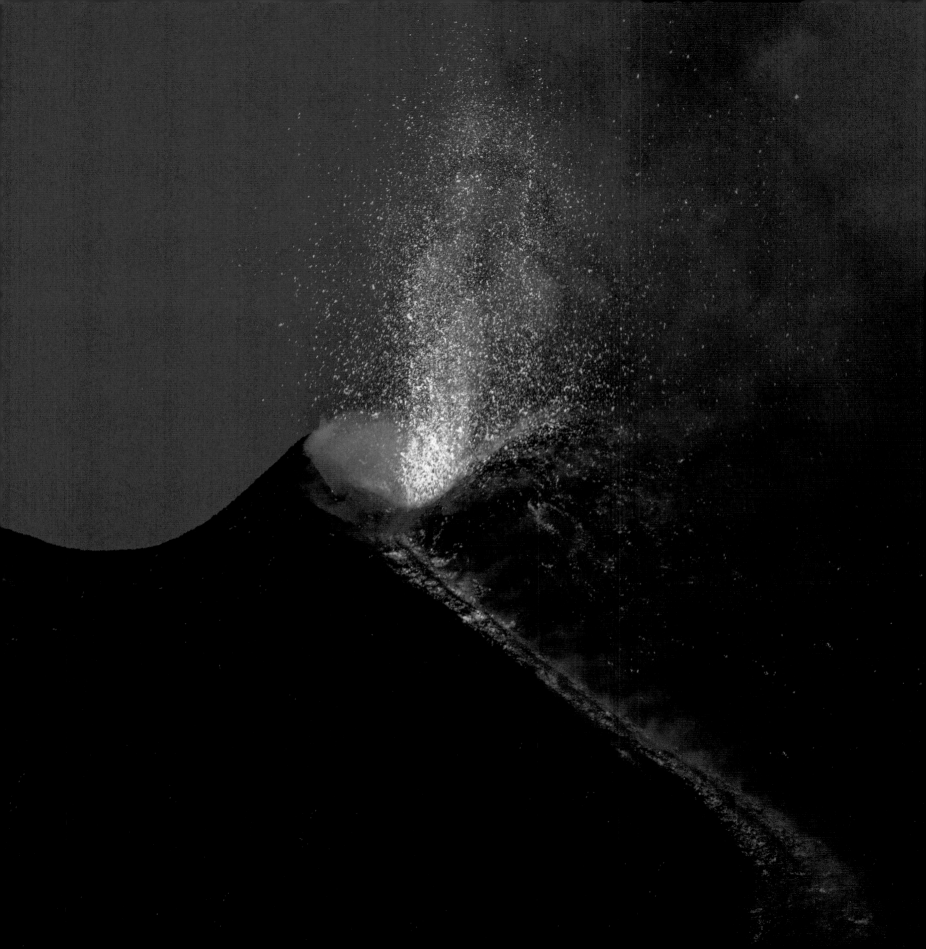

Sometimes the Inside of the Earth Comes Out

Beneath the thin earth's crust is a thick, boiling liquid of stone and rubble, which we call **magma.** Fortunately, the thin earth's crust is strong enough to hold this bubbling magma in its place. But occasionally, the earth's crust tears, causing the magma to spill out as **lava.** Volcanoes occur wherever the earth's crust bursts. During an eruption, the lava, ash, and debris can be thrown half a mile into the air!

Eruption Etna, Italy

Not All Volcanoes are the Same

There are about **1,500 volcanoes** in the world, and they're all different. While one volcano might be life–threatening, another might be slow–moving and mild.

The most dangerous volcano is recognized by its shape. Its slopes are steep with several internal rivers through which magma tries to enter. But the rock of this so-called stratovolcano is incredibly strong, trapping the boiling magma. Once it escapes, there's a massive **eruption.**

Other volcanoes, such as the shield volcano, are flat. These volcanoes are formed in places where the earth's crust is very thin. Here, the magma can escape more easily. Sometimes the lava slowly flows over the earth like a thick, hot soup. Eruptions are much less common in these types of volcanoes.

Sinabung, Indonesia

Eruption Etna, Italy

The Power of Nature

The power of volcanoes can't be contained, but it can be detected. Scientists are able to use **seismographs** to detect the rumbling in the ground. These convert the vibrations in the ground into graphs. Thanks to seismographs, many people escape volcanic eruptions.

The Eruption of the Krakatoa

The eruption of the Krakatoa volcano in Indonesia in 1883 was so loud that even people in Australia heard it! The explosion also released a huge amount of dust. The dust cloud flew all over the world and even clouded the sun! As a result, the temperature decreased in many countries.

The Ash Cloud of Eyjafjallajökull

Iceland is home to the Eyjafjallajökull volcano, which recently erupted. The ash cloud that was released during its eruption spread over a large part of Europe. With an impact up to 5 miles high, the air filled with ash particles. Aircraft had to stay on the ground for nearly a month!

In the year 79, the inhabitants of the Roman city of Pompeii were startled by a loud rumbling. The volcano Vesuvius, which was located just outside the city, erupted with great violence. It rained hot ashes. The entire city was buried under a thick layer of dust. Hundreds of years later, Pompeii was excavated and under the ashes were the houses, shops, and bathhouses just as they had been left by the Romans more than a thousand years earlier!

Rivers of Lava

In **Hawaii,** there's a volcano right on the earth's surface. The lava flows like a river across the island. It's of course very hot, but it flows so slowly that many people can witness its beauty.

New Land

Many islands are the result of volcanic eruptions at the bottom of the sea. The lava then flows into the cool water and solidifies. This is how volcanic islands begin.

Lava is dangerous, but once it cools, it can also be useful. Cooled lava is very **fertile.** Plants thrive on it!

Souvenir from the Inside of the Earth

People have never traveled beneath the earth's crust. It's so hot there that everything melts: steel, stones, hard diamonds . . . everything! How can we see what's **just below the earth's crust?** We can look at lava! It comes from deep parts of the earth. Lava is actually a souvenir from inside of the earth.

The Center of the Earth

Our journey to the center of the earth has reached its destination: the core. The core is mostly hidden. Although we've sent satellites to planets like Mars, Saturn, and Jupiter, we haven't been able to send a measuring instrument to the core of the earth. But thanks to scientists, we can learn a lot about the **earth's core.**

The center of the earth is exactly 3,958 miles below your feet. That's just a little more than the distance between New York and London, or between Beijing and Moscow. The core consists of two parts: a liquid outer core and a solid inner core. The core is made up of metal, which is completely melted by the heat, but is completely compressed into a solid ball. How strange it is to think that the temperature in the core is as hot as the temperature on the surface of the sun!

The Earth's Core is Like a Magnet

The core of the earth consists largely of iron, and it works like a large magnet. This **super magnet** has influence all over the world! The magnetic field, for example, is the basis for the compass. Because of the magnetic effect, the needles of all compasses, wherever you are, point in the same direction: north. The magnetic field can even be felt outside the earth, and when the sun emits electrically charged particles, the field becomes visible. Around the North Pole and South Pole, the magnetic field deflects light particles. When it's dark, you can clearly see which patterns they produce. Sometimes the northern or southern lights consist of a light glow, and sometimes curtains of light. The dancing curtains display all the colors of the rainbow—a result of the core's magnetic effect.

Ershfjord, Norway

Index